Philosophy of War

Philosophy of War

A Brief Analysis on Principles and Justifications

Joel Steele

RESOURCE *Publications* • Eugene, Oregon

PHILOSOPHY OF WAR
A Brief Analysis on Principles and Justifications

Copyright © 2020 Joel Steele. All rights reserved. Except for brief quotations in critical publications or reviews, no part of this book may be reproduced in any manner without prior written permission from the publisher. Write: Permissions, Wipf and Stock Publishers, 199 W. 8th Ave., Suite 3, Eugene, OR 97401.

Resource Publications
An Imprint of Wipf and Stock Publishers
199 W. 8th Ave., Suite 3
Eugene, OR 97401

www.wipfandstock.com

PAPERBACK ISBN: 978-1-7252-8526-2
HARDCOVER ISBN: 978-1-7252-8527-9
EBOOK ISBN: 978-1-7252-8528-6

Manufactured in the U.S.A.   09/18/20

"Such is War: such the commander who conducts it; such the theory which rules it. But War is no past time; no mere passion for venturing and winning; no work of a free enthusiasm; it is a serious means for a serious object."

—CLAUSEWITZ

Contents

Preface | ix
Introduction | xi

1. The Peloponnesian War | 1
2. The World Wars | 7
3. The Soviet-Afghan War | 20

Bibliography | 33

Preface

THIS ANALYSIS DRAWS ON theories from three theorists—Carl von Clausewitz, Sun-tzu, and Thomas Aquinas—for insights into theories on war and justifications for waging war. Although Thomas Aquinas is known more for his contributions to theology and philosophy, he was included in this project because his ideas pertaining to "just war" have a semblance of theory. The theoretical and philosophical contributions developed by these three theorists are used to evaluate specifically chosen wars across a broad historical spectrum; they include: the Peloponnesian War, the World Wars, and the Soviet-Afghan War. A historiography of the literature for each war is provided, followed by an evaluation through the lens of the three theorists. Primary sources were used to extract information regarding the chosen wars; these include: Thucydides, John Keynes, the Treaty of Versailles, State Department Bureau of Public Affairs, The Russian General Staff, and the memoirs of Vladislav Tamarov, published in his book, *Afghanistan: A Russian Soldier's Story*. The primary sources extracted from the theories come from the theorists' own publications; they include: *On War*, by Clausewitz; *Summa Theologica*, by Thomas Aquinas; and *The Art of War*, attributed to Sun-tzu. The theories pertaining to war developed by Clausewitz, Sun-tzu, and Aquinas are not constrained by time periods; they are applicable to the past, present, and future. The properties from which the theories consist have always existed within humanity, but it took certain minds to extrapolate through observations their place among civilizations as they evolved and clashed.

Introduction

THE ACT OF WAR has simultaneously produced horrific conditions for civilizations and created the possibility of liberation for those bound by forced inhumane suffering brought on by their oppressors. Clausewitz, one of the greatest theorists to write about war, argued that no sensible man starts a war, or at least he should not do so, without having a clear vision as to what he intends to achieve and how he intends to conduct it.[1] Sun-tzu, if he ever actually existed, also wrote theories on war, or at least these ancient theories we have are credited to this historical actor. Nonetheless, Sun-tzu's and Clausewitz's theories are studied by military institutions all over the world. According to Clausewitz, "War therefore is an act of violence intended to compel our opponent to fulfill our will."[2] Society has an understanding of what defines war. However, the conditions in which a society is justified for initiating war are less agreeable. Military power and military development, on a global scale, seem to have challenged civilized political systems, forcing them to strike a balance between the destructiveness of warfare and providing a strong deterrence against radical entities set on waging war. This is not an easy task. However, there is an available standard developed from the best Western sources.

Thomas Aquinas developed a justification for waging war that he extracted from the Greek philosopher Aristotle, Christian theology, and Scripture. It can be summed up by focusing on three

1. Strachan, *Clausewitz's On War*, 3.
2. Clausewitz, *On War*, 3.

Introduction

things: First, war does not belong to the private citizen, therefore only rulers charged with protecting the commonwealth have the moral authority to initiate war by calling upon the state's citizens. Second, the enemy must deserve to have war waged on them because of some act of evil they have inflicted (just cause). And third, the rulers who wage war must have the right intentions—to promote good while suppressing evil, never for the purpose of gain but to preserve righteousness.[3] This study will analyze the theoretical and philosophical contributions developed by those who have profoundly influenced theories pertaining to war and how it should be conducted. It will be approached through the evaluation of specified wars across a vast stretch of history, disclosing insights into the theories that guide strategists who participate in this aberration.

Carl von Clausewitz

Carl von Clausewitz was born in a small town southwest of Berlin. His father had a Protestant background and his mother's family managed a royal farm. The army accepted Clausewitz and his two brothers as officer cadets after the death of Frederick the Great—who insisted the officer corps be reserved for nobility. Clausewitz and his brothers all became generals; they entered the nobility through the church and service in the army of the Prussian state.[4] In 1792, Clausewitz enlisted in the Prussian Army and assisted the First Coalition against Revolutionary France. In 1801, he was accepted into the Institute for Young Officers. Some of his basic ideas on the theory of war were formed during the three years he spent at the institute. Clausewitz participated in the Battle of Jena-Auestadt in 1806, and spent time in French captivity when Napoleon defeated the Prussians in a decisive battle. After his release in 1807, he joined a group of middle-ranking officers who attempted to reform the Prussian army. In an effort to preserve Prussia, this group of reformers adapted a trait from the Revolutionary French,

3. Aquinas, *Summa Theologica*, 165.
4. Paret, "Clausewitz," 188.

Introduction

that is, a mass enlistment tactic. Clausewitz secured a position in the war ministry that was headed by Gerhard Johann David von Scharnhorst. He looked for an opportunity to wage a national war of liberation on France and became frustrated by the king's hesitation to act. In 1812, Clausewitz resigned his commission in response to Prussia being forced to join Napoleon; he then joined the Russian army to help resist the Napoleon invasion of Russia. He was assigned many posts and after the French retreat he was involved in persuading the Prussians to change sides.[5] As peace approached Prussia, Clausewitz decided to revisit his theories on war first developed at the Institute for Young Officers. His position as head of the Military Academy at Berlin enabled him to focus on his work regarding the theory of war. In 1831, Clausewitz was appointed Chief of Staff to the Prussian army as they prepared to intervene in the Polish Revolt. He died of cholera that same year.[6]

Clausewitz believed a general theory of war was comprehensible. However, unlike the military thinkers of the Enlightenment, he did not believe the theory of war should be based on rules and principles and given a mathematical form because human affairs and war are more complex than a natural phenomenon occurring within the sciences.[7] Clausewitz developed goals he deemed essential to obtain. He applied the study of mathematics and philosophical methods to social, political, and military action. However, this approach by itself was inadequate. Thus, to understand politics, war, and society with clarity, Clausewitz sought to understand them through observation and by searching for their true purpose and interconnections. To accomplish this, he embarked on an historical study, with the help of Scharnhorst.[8] This educational journey had a profound impact on Clausewitz and the development of his theories pertaining to war. Historian Peter Paret disclosed a letter written to Clausewitz by his mentor Scharnhorst who emphasizes the importance of an independent

---

5. *Britannica Academic*, s.v. "Carl von Clausewitz," para. 3.
6. *Britannica Academic*, s.v. "Carl von Clausewitz," para. 1.
7. *Britannica Academic*, s.v. "Carl von Clausewitz," para. 2.
8. Paret, "Clausewitz," 400.

Introduction

nation achieved through education and encouraging the people to take charge of their own affairs.⁹ This illustrates the various views from which primary intellectual thought is forged by the theorist's own individual experiences. Many historians believe balanced interpretations of *On War* are rare and often are not in the context of Clausewitz's age. To put them in the context of Clausewitz's age, the historian must consider the influences of Clausewitz's early life. His concern for education and improving the individual becomes the source for his politics and theories developed through his studies on philosophy, history, and literature. This is essential for determining the relevance of Clausewitz's theories as they pertain to modern warfare. Moreover, that is why the decision was made to include a slightly more extensive background on Clausewitz, compared to the other three theorists in this study.

Clausewitz on Technology and Friction

Military strategist David J. Lonsdale explains how modern technology further enhances some of Clausewitz's theories. Lonsdale contends modern warfare can apply to and further develop Clausewitz's theories as technology advances. For example, friction can be better managed with the help of air support. Most importantly, "the political process must be able to adapt to setbacks that inevitably flow from the presence of friction in the conduct of war."¹⁰ Air support is a component of war that helps reduce friction and reach the primary objective in war. Other supportive theories on war developed from Clausewitz's theories as well. From the nineteenth century through the beginning of the twentieth century, there emerged theories on naval warfare that proved to be the most successful of any past century and which would extend well into the future. Two of the most influential naval warfare theorists during this era were British naval historian Julian Corbett and

---

9. Paret, "Clausewitz," 404.

10. Lonsdale, "Ordering and Controlling the Dimensions of Strategy," 399–400.

Introduction

American Rear Admiral Alfred Mahan.[11] Of the two, Corbett was the one most influenced by Clausewitz. Corbett's theory is about study not action, but in order to succeed a commander needs to be decisive in his actions and communicate his intentions to others. Thus, a theory is useful if a commander can communicate through language that is understandable by all—using precise language to be contemplated during training and assessed after an action. According to Corbett, a theory can also provide intellectual tools needed to contemplate decisions made by politicians in high-pressure situations where immediate action is required. A theory, Corbett suggests, will also serve to bridge communications between statesmen and military officers to assist them in understanding the aspects of the conflict they are about to engage in.[12]

The influence Clausewitz had on Corbett is evident in his ideas regarding the supportive components of war. Corbett viewed sea power as instrumental to the advancement of the larger purpose of war, but naval power is not an end in itself. Clausewitz believed war was conducted to achieve a political goal. Corbett's theory and writings reflect this same premise, viewing the Navy's role as support for the larger objective in war and to protect national interests. Corbett finds it important to study war and develop theories for educational purposes but agrees with Clausewitz that even the best theory on war is no substitute for experience and judgment. Theories on war cannot be systematically condensed into an exact science; they can, however, show reoccurring patterns and complexities that are consistent and can be expected in war. For example, friction and chance can always be expected, and while advances in technology may be beneficial for limiting them, they will never be completely eliminated.[13] Corbett disagrees with Clausewitz on limited war. Clausewitz does not advocate for limited war, in contrast, Corbett does believe there are advantages to limited war. Clausewitz writes about "The Battle" in *On War*: "A conflict of the main body, but not an unimportant one about a

11. Widen "Sir Julian Corbett and the Theoretical Study of War," 109.
12. Widen "Sir Julian Corbett and the Theoretical Study of War," 112–13.
13. Handel, "Corbett, Clausewitz, and Sun Tzu," 109.

Introduction

secondary object, not a mere attempt which is given up when we see betimes that are object is hardly within our reach: it is a conflict waged with all our forces for the attainment of a decisive victory." Describing the distinctive characteristics of war, he continues . . . "it is undertaken with the sole purpose of obtaining a decisive victory."[14] Corbett does not believe this strategy is best suited for naval warfare; he believes the concentration of forces has done more harm than good at sea. The factors at sea produce conditions too complex for such obtuse solutions. Corbett's primary defense for his theory of limited engagement is a comparison of sea and land conditions: it is harder for the superior fleet to manipulate conditions and thus force an inferior fleet to engage because it is easier for the enemy's fleet at sea to avoid conflict than it is for the army on land. Moreover, a concentration of forces weakens the fleet's positions in other areas of strategic importance, making them vulnerable for counterattack.[15] Naval and maritime operations will be an important factor in the first chapter of this study, titled "The Peloponnesian War."

Thomas Aquinas

Thomas Aquinas developed many key aspects in Christian theology. He is best known for his argument "Five Ways," which was evidence for the existence of God.[16] Aquinas also contributed to theology regarding the image of God. He believed the image of God was located in a person's soul.[17] He also viewed the natural world as a place of divine presence. For Aquinas, God is present in all of creation, although God is not a substance of his creation. The only creatures made in the image of God are intelligent or spiritual, with the capacity to know God and receive his wisdom. Humans are the only creatures in God's creation to fit these criteria. The

---

14. Clausewitz, *On War*, 227.
15. Handel, "Corbett, Clausewitz, and Sun Tzu," 109.
16. McGrath, *Historical Theology*, 91.
17. "Image of God," 28.

Introduction

intellectual life, according to Aquinas, focuses on reason and will, leading to a shift in the image of God in humanity. The relation between intelligence that allows for the capacity of speech and the development of ideas unites reason with will to produce free will, thereby placing the image of God in the power of humans to act morally responsible. For example, free will, according to Aquinas, is progressively formed in humans to produce moral acts consistent with the image of God. The freedom developed in this process is imperfect, that is, free will agents can still engage in deviant behavior, but as the process continues and humans make an effort to conform to the image of God, the stronger the will becomes to deny sinful acts.[18] Thus, humans have the capacity to make ethical choices that correspond to the image of God.

Humanity's morality and motives for seeking justice are the byproduct of God's creation that originated when humans were created in God's image. The moral code that dwells in humanity was installed at creation.[19] A key issue or problem regarding morality with respect to contemporary culture is the source of morality. For Aquinas, the source is clearly God. However, for those who reject God, articulating moral obligations becomes difficult. A popular view in secular society for explaining moral obligations is that of cultural relativism. The philosophy behind cultural relativism views moral obligations in terms of social approvals and disapprovals. For example, the actions deemed acceptable for a given culture within society will be taught and indoctrinated into the youth of that culture. Hence, action designated right or wrong will vary from culture to culture. Moreover, in a society that adheres to cultural relativism, there exists no transcendent moral obligations for humans because an objectifiable source does not exist.[20] This creates a serious problem for cultural relativism. Since there does not exist a higher moral authority for evaluating the value of an action, a culture that practices infanticide, racism, or genocide could not be condemned by other cultures that did not practice such actions. By rejecting objectivity,

---

18. Pinckaers et al., "Ethics and the Image of God," 34, 37–38.
19. Erickson, *Christian Theology*, 257.
20. Evans and Manis, *Philosophy of Religion*, 89.

xvii

Introduction

God, or Aquinas's claim that humanity was created in the image of God, which was integrated at creation, it allows for the possibility of a destructive culture within society. For example, the moral beliefs and practices of Nazi Germany could not be criticized by other cultures under the philosophy of cultural relativism.[21] However, when a culture secures an objectifiable source as the standard to evaluate its morality, the need for moral change becomes apparent. Aquinas's doctrine pertaining to the image of God is essential for understanding his developments on "just war."

Sun-tzu

Sun-tzu's *Military Strategy*, best known as the *Art of War*, is the most popular Chinese strategy pertaining to war in the West. There are rumors that early Western leaders such as Napoleon and members of the Nazi High Command have studied it. For Asia, however, it has been the most important military document on strategy. According to Ralph D. Sawyer, translator and commentator on *The Seven Military Classics of Ancient China*, the Chinese regard it as the oldest and most influential source, dated toward the end of the six century BC.[22] This military treatise can be enigmatic and debates have ensued over whether Sun-tzu, a single person, was the composer of all the material. Thus, only a brief introduction will be provided. Nevertheless, there exists aspects from Sun-tzu's theories which are clear regarding philosophical principles on war. The primary focus is on manipulating the enemy through exploitation and various tactics to weaken, frustrate, and exhaust your opponent before attacking. Deceit, trickery, and deception are fundamental to its philosophy. All these strategies revolve around a common goal: to defeat the enemy without engaging in direct armed combat. Diplomacy is the preferred method.[23] It has been said that, in the West, war is a continuation of policy, but in Sun-tzu's view, war is a failure of policy.

21. Evans and Manis, *Philosophy of Religion*, 90.
22. Sawyer, *Seven Military Classics of Ancient China*, 149.
23. Sawyer, *Seven Military Classics of Ancient China*, 154–55.

1

The Peloponnesian War

ATHENS'S RISE TO DOMINANCE in the fifth century was primarily attributed to their Navy. They controlled most of the Mediterranean through approximation to location, that is, out of the 179 states the most remote was within a 200–250-mile range from Athens (an eight-day voyage by sea). Still, they did not go unchallenged. The militarized πόλις (*polis*), that is, city-state, of Sparta organized the Peloponnesian League to engage in a series of land and sea conflicts known as the Peloponnesian War. Athens became overextended as the skirmishes prolonged. Athens's empire weakened as they lost land after a series of defeats, and in 446 BC they were forced to negotiated a peace. In the winter of 446–445, Athens and Sparta officially agreed on a Thirty Years Peace arrangement. This resulted in two great powers in the ancient world that would remain suspicious of each other until the Second Peloponnesian War broke out in 431.[1]

Sparta was unique. They had conquered their neighbors, the helots, and subjected them to the forceful service of the state, a form of serfdom. The helots provided food for the Spartans by farming the land. This liberated the Spartans from mundane tedious labor enabling them to engage in continuous military training from age seven and serving until age sixty when military

1. Carey, *Warfare in the Ancient World*, 51.

service was no longer a requirement. The alliances Sparta formed with surrounding city-states required them to serve under Spartan command when needed, swearing allegiance to have the same friends and enemies as Spartan in return for the great power's protection.[2] Spartan's style of government was complex; it contained monarchic, oligarchic, and democratic elements. An elected council of men over sixty, chosen from privileged families, represented the oligarchic element; an assembly of men over the age of thirty represented the democratic element; and two kings that served for life represented the monarchic element.[3]

Athens had a unique history as well. Athens emerged as the world's first democratic-style government in the fifth century. Democracy for Athens depended on its maritime empire. During the Persian War, Athenian allies of the Greek city-states invited Athens to take the initiative in the fight for liberation against the Persians. Nearly all members of the Athenian alliance ceased maritime operations, electing to pay into a centralized treasury associated with the alliance which would fund Athens's Navy and maritime operations. The decision to redirect all funds to the Athenian Navy resulted in the largest and best naval force the world had known. The powerful Athenian Navy provided protection for their merchant ships beyond the Mediterranean.[4] After the Persian War, Athens rebuilt their walls around the city and their large empire became concerning for the Spartans. If fact, Sparta protested Athens's desire to rebuild their walls. However, the walls went up with no regard for the Spartans' opposition. The Spartans remained embittered and resentful of Athens's powerful empire. Nevertheless, they made no additional complaints.[5]

2. Kagan, *On the Origins of War*, 20.
3. Kagan, *On the Origins of War*, 21.
4. Kagan, *On the Origins of War*, 24–25.
5. Kagan, *On the Origins of War*, 27.

The Peloponnesian War

Belligerent Allies and Fear

One of many problems with weaker sovereign allies is the possibility of them dragging their greater, much more capable ally into a major conflict with an opposing great power. This scenario materialized for the Spartans when one of their allies, Corinth, became embroiled in a dispute with Corcyra. The Corcyraeans' Navy was second only to that of Athens. However, the Corcyraeans feared the Corinthians would enlist the help of other alliances within the Spartan league. The Corcyraeans were neutral and did not have an alliance with either of the two great opposing powers, Sparta and Athens. Thus, once the Corcyraeans realized the Corinthians were determined to wage war, the Corcyraeans sought the help of the Athenians. The provisions of the Thirty-Years'-Peace Treaty, ratified in 446–45, allowed for neutral powers to join the alliances of either of the two great powers. So, Athens would have been within the confines of the treaty to accept the Corcyraeans' request for assistance. Moreover, the Corcyraeans appealed to Athens's fears, arguing that if they succumbed to the Corinthians their fleet would fall into the control of the Spartan league.[6] This would present a major challenge to Athenian maritime power in the region, tipping the balance of power in Sparta's favor. Still, caution was needed to avoid unintentionally setting off a premature war with the Spartans.

Historian Donald Kagan provides a detailed account of the events that led to the Peloponnesian War in his book, *On the Origins of War*. Kagan delivers a superb narrative of the tactics used by Corinth and the Corcyraeans to persuade the two great powers to choose a side. This account will be brief because understanding the psychology of the ancients is problematic. It becomes more problematic when modern researchers attempt to understand motivations that extend beyond what has been recorded by those closest to the event, or to speculate on surviving artifacts, forcing them to fit a supportive testimony. The focus will be on what occurred and how those actions fit into a general theory of war and justification developed by one or more of the three theorists introduced at the beginning of this study.

---

6. Kagan, *On the Origins of War*, 42–43.

Philosophy of War

After some debate—mostly rhetoric, embellishment, and hyperbole—the two belligerent city-states had stirred the fears of both the Spartans and Athenians. As previously stated, Athens was cautious. Thus, they decided to send only ten warships to the area rather than a large armada, as presumably this would be less likely to provoke Sparta. Essentially, the Athenians made an alliance with the Corcyraeans that was defensive only. The Greek general Pericles was most likely behind this idea. There are two primary sources used for this interpretation: Plutarch and Thucydides. Kagan explores this in *On the Origins of War*, but he argues against Thucydides's claim that the Athenians voted for the treaty with Corcyra because they viewed a war with Sparta as inevitable (Kagan's argument against Thucydides's interpretation is found in his earlier publication, *The Outbreak of the Peloponnesian War*).[7] Nevertheless, Corinth initiated war with Corcyra assuming the Athenians would stand aside. With the help of a few colonies and allies the Corinthians attacked the Corcyraeans' fleet in September of 433.[8]

The Corcyraeans had 110 warships, and the Corinthians, combined with their allies, had 150 warships. It wasn't long before the Corinthians gained the advantage and began to press the Corcyraeans. The Athenians realized they could no longer stand by, so they engaged the Corinthians. However, the Corinthians noticed an Athenian fleet of twenty new warships. Apparently, a fierce debate ensued among the Athenians after the first ten ships left for the region and more ships were dispatched to the area. Not knowing how many ships could be over the horizon or en route, the Corinthians decided to disengage. The next day the Corinthians pulled out of the area because they worried Athens would consider the skirmish the beginning of a full-on war.[9] Corinth could not win a war against Athens without the support of Sparta. The Athenians allowed them to leave peacefully. The minimal effort plan (defensive only) had failed and Athens now had to prepare for war.[10]

7. Kagan, *On the Origins of War*, 43–45.
8. Kagan, *On the Origins of War*, 47.
9. Thucydides, *Peloponnesian War*, 24–27.
10. Thucydides, *Peloponnesian War*, 48.

The Peloponnesian War

Comparing the Theories

Athens ended up losing the war. The focus from this point will be on the details and action which had the most impact. There are distinct actions during the Peloponnesian War which Clausewitz's theories warn against. None of Aquinas's theories on "just war" were considered by Sparta or Athens, as fear and suspicion ruled both sides. Perhaps Sun-tzu's concept regarding a failure in politics holds true, i.e., war is a consequence of failed political negotiations. Of course, with the exception of Sun-tzu (around 512 BC) these theories had not been developed,[11] but that's not the point. It's important to realize these theories were chosen because they are not constrained by time periods in the past or the future. They do not function like applications relevant to the current technology of the era but they are properties of a continuity derived from complex human experiences extending back to at least the beginning of civilization. As previously indicated, these properties from which the theories were realized have always existed within humanity; it simply took certain minds to recognize and articulate their place as warfare persisted in advanced civilizations.

Clausewitz's goal was to explain war as a universal phenomenon.[12] His theory on war involved universal principles that could apply to war itself. In this sense the theory holds true regarding past and future warfare. Clausewitz viewed war as a tool to accomplish political goals; technology does not alter this reality in modern warfare. In book eight, chapter two of *On War*, Clausewitz states, "the overthrow of the enemy is the natural end of the act of war; and if we would keep within the strictly philosophical limits of the idea, there can be no other in reality."[13] These ideas apply to ancient warfare as well. Another important concept from Clausewitz's theories was the idea of "absolute war." He insisted a war with no limits, absolute war, is the only war in which armies should engage and that limited war should only be limited by nature, not by

11. Sawyer, *Seven Military Classics of China*, 149.
12. Strachan, *Clausewitz's On War*, 77.
13. Clausewitz, *On War*, 666.

choice. A good example of war limited by nature is natural barriers that would prevent access to adequately engage with the enemy, or impassible terrain—mountains, swamps, rivers, etc.[14] This concept will become more apparent in the Soviet-Afghan War section of this analysis.

The Athenians were reluctant to agree to a full alliance with the Corcyraeans; instead they elected to take a limited position—defensive alliance only. In his book Kagan contemplates Athens's decision to practice limited warfare. Kagan hypothesizes, "perhaps a full offensive and defensive alliance such as the Corcyraeans proposed would have convinced the Corinthians that Athens was serious."[15] Nevertheless, when Sparta and Athens went to war the Athenians took mostly a defensive position. These two actions proved to be not only a violation of Clausewitz's theories but the primary factors contributing to Athens's defeat. Sun-tzu's theory on war was to subjugate your enemy without actually engaging in combat. He emphasized diplomacy and coercion to manipulate and frustrate the enemy, and to only resort to armed combat when the enemy threatens the state with military action.[16] Diplomacy had failed but Athens continued to employ a defensive strategy. Aquinas's principles on the justification for war were also ignored. Neither side was guilty of inflicting evil on the other, therefore, neither side had justification to wage war. The Athenians and Spartans were influenced by fear and suspicion of each other, magnified by their allies' rhetoric. Both parties were, however, concerned with gaining influence and power in the region if for no other reason than to check the power and influence of the other. This was another infringement of Aquinas's principles—never engage in war for the purpose of gain.

---

14. Clausewitz, *On War*, 452–59, 474–89, 493–98, 666–669.
15. Kagan, *On the Origins of War*, 74.
16. Sawyer, *Seven Military Classics of China*, 154.

2

The World Wars

THE INDUSTRIAL REVOLUTION WAS a unique period in history. The change it brought was perhaps never experienced more fully than by those who participated in the Great War of 1914–18. The rapid escalation to the theatre of war—industrialized, automatic, long-range weapons—created technological conditions that required a reorganization of command within the military. Junior officers were forced to take on more responsibility as battles could no longer be fought under the supervision of a single commander. All European infantry rifles were sighted at 1,000 yards and artillery, made mobile by rail and roads, had a range of twenty-five miles. Soldiers would therefore experience the enemy's fire long before they could see them.[1]

The First World War lasted more than four years, creating horrible conditions for all involved. The Allied losses were: 5.4 million dead and 7 million wounded. The Central Powers' losses totaled 4 million dead and 8.3 million wounded. Millions of citizens from both sides died from causes directly and indirectly associated with the war.[2] Initially, Americans did not want to get involved in the war "over there"; they viewed the conflict as a European war that should not involve America. American corporations,

---

1. Howard, *First World War,* 16–17.
2. Kagan et al., *Western Heritage,* 867.

however, viewed the war as a chance to make additional profits while expanding American economic influence through financial services and other materials. Woodrow Wilson took up the task of devising polices that would allow Americans to benefit financially from the war while keeping them out of it.³ Wilson's primary objective was for the U.S. to retain the moral authority and capacity of ending the war through mediation while establishing a new world order. He believed America was charged with saving Western civilization and rebuilding European nations after war had torn them apart. Thus, Wilson overlooked America making money from the war as contradictory to neutrality.⁴ This section covers what caused a nation and its leader to abandon their strongly held position on neutrality and replace it instead with belligerence.

Wilson had the foresight to know the war would be an important opportunity for the United States. Although Wilson did truly hope the war would end through negotiations implemented by the U.S., the claim of neutrality was a fallacy to benefit his political career, American corporations, and the American economy. There are several events and actions that support this claim. For instance, on April 2, Wilson was reelected because of the sentiment that "he kept us out of the war," but five months later he asked Congress for a declaration of war on Germany.⁵ The United States overlooked the British illegal blockade that restricted Germany from obtaining material needed for survival. Further, they warned Germany not to engage in submarine warfare that would put American citizens at risk, knowing British merchant ships used the ruse of flying neutral flags.⁶ Following the Lusitania event, another ship was destroyed by a German U-boat that resulted in two American lives lost. Consequently, the Germans pledged to announce attacks on merchant and passenger ships which would have allowed personnel to exit a ship before it was sunk. The Wilson administration disregarded the pledge(s) and they continued to make policies that

3. Zieger, *America's Great War*, 16–18.
4. Zieger, *America's Great War*, 51.
5. Hanlon, "America's Turn from Neutrality to Intervention," 1.
6. Zieger, *America's Great War*, 23, 41.

The World Wars

would put them on a path toward entering the war by allowing private citizens to dictate America's policy regarding war through their irresponsible decisions to travel through war zones.[7] So, neutrality was a fallacy. Indeed, Wilson's initial plan was to keep America out of the war but assessing his actions will demonstrate he was not neutral.

What persuaded Wilson to commit American troops to the European war? The role played by American financiers, specifically the House of Morgan, is crucial for understanding Wilson's change from his professed position of neutrality to bellicosity. The structure of the House of Morgan during World War I consisted of: J. P. Morgan & Co. in New York, Morgan Grenfell & Co. in London, Drexel & Co. in Philadelphia, and Morgan-Harjes in Paris. Morgan banks worked diligently to supply the Allies with loans to further their cause.[8] Once it was clear the war was not going to end soon, the French and British governments appointed J. P. Morgan & Co. purchasing agent in the United States.[9] In 1915, a syndicate of banks led by J. P. Morgan issued a loan of $500 million to the Allies before America entered the war.[10] The allies became heavily reliant on loans which allowed J. P. Morgan & Co. to control French and British financial policy. In addition to coordinating Allied loans in the U.S., J. P. Morgan & Co. was providing an overdraft exceeding $100 million to the Allies. Neither London nor Paris were happy with a private bank wielding control over their finances. However, both struggled to find alternative options. Relationships became strained between the Allies, specifically the French, as they sunk deeper into debt. The House of Morgan and the Allies relied on each other at this point because a disruption in credit would cause irreparable damage to the Allies and endanger the bank.[11]

There is speculation that the Zimmerman Telegram or the sinking of American merchant ships caused Wilson to change his

---

7. Zieger, *America's Great War*, 25, 41.
8. Horn, "Private Bank at War," 85.
9. Horn, "Private Bank at War," 86.
10. Horn, "Private Bank at War," 100.
11. Horn, "Private Bank at War," 105–6.

mind.[12] However, these were past occurrences that could have been dealt with when they took place. Further, the Germans made pledges that seemed to lessen Wilson's outrage. It was not until the Germans realized Wilson had no intention of addressing the British illegal blockade that they engaged in unrestricted submarine warfare. Even so, Wilson credited the German government with honorable intentions and there was nothing to indicate America was in danger of an attack from Germany. In fact, is was in Germany's best interest for the Americans to stay neutral, a concept they well understood as indicated by their intentions. Wilson's sudden conversion to war derives from the growing risks faced by the House of Morgan and other financial interests. Indeed, in some ways it was a call to war "at the command of gold," and Wilson presented a case for war, (through carefully crafted speeches and propaganda) the American people would accept with enthusiasm.[13] In 1936, J. P. Morgan Jr. was called before the Munitions Senate Committee to answer questions regarding currency manipulation. The committee wanted to know if Morgan intentionally took measures that triggered the British pound exchange rate slump, forcing Wilson to alter his policy of neutrality. Morgan angrily denied the allegations.[14] Nevertheless, prior to the war the United States was a debtor nation. However, they emerged as the strongest financial country in the world and J. P. Morgan continued to benefit extensively after the war as European countries required loans to rebuild.[15]

The Peace and Prelude to Greater Destruction

The most common understanding as to what caused the Second World War is when the Germans invaded Poland on September 1, 1939. However, to find out what led to the conditions that put a leader like Hitler into power you would have to go back to Paris

12. Brown, "Initially Reluctant, U.S.," 29.
13. Zieger, *America's Great War*, 52–54.
14. Special to *The New York Times*, "J. P. Morgan Denies Letting the Pound Slip," 1–2.
15. Horn, "Private Bank at War," 86.

at the end of World War I, to the Treaty of Versailles. The German Weimar Republic was created after the defeat of the imperial army. Its name came from the city of Weimar, where its constitution was written in 1919. During the same period the constitution was being debated the Republic was forced to sign the Treaty of Versailles under threat of invasion by Allied forces. From that point the Weimar Republic was associated with the humiliating terms of the agreement. Borrowing money to pay its war debts, Germany's inflation became a major problem after WWI. Printing presses had difficulty keeping up with the rise of prices. During this time Germany's currency was the mark and it was not worth the paper it was printed on due to hyperinflation. Many stores were unwilling to exchange goods for the worthless money. Germans did not believe they were solely responsible for the war and deeply resented the unbearable demands that were written into the treaty. An extreme economic burden, loss of territory, and a weak republic allowed Hitler to take office.[16]

The Fourteen Points introduced by Woodrow Wilson allowed nationalities the right to self-determination. However, it was difficult to draw a map in Europe to match ethnic groups with their homelands.[17] Wilson's main objective at the peace conference was to create a new world order under the entity the League of Nations.[18] Germany was excluded from the peace conference; they were presented with a treaty and expected to accept it. The treaty had been dictated and some believed it was immoral and unworkable economically for the Germans. British economist John Maynard Keynes participated in the peace conference. He was one of the biggest critics of the treaty, referring to it as a "Carthaginian peace." Keynes believed the treaty would bring economic ruin and war to Europe.[19]

France and Britain expected Germany to pay the full cost of the war. In addition to the $15–$20 billion the Americans

---

16. Kagan et al., *Western Heritage*, 867.
17. Kagan et al., *Western Heritage*, 865.
18. Howard, *First World War*, 113.
19. Keynes, *Economic Consequences of Peace*, ch. 4, para. 2.

Philosophy of War

proposed, they wanted pensions to be paid to survivors and dependents. Most agreed Germany would not be able to pay these huge sums, whatever they may be. In the meantime, Germany was to pay $5 billion annually until 1921. A final figure would then be set and paid out over a thirty-year period. To justify these huge settlements the Allies inserted a war guilt clause into the treaty[20]:

> The Allied and Associated Governments affirm and Germany accepts the responsibility of Germany and her allies for causing all the loss and damage to which the Allied and Associated Governments and their nationals have been subjected as a consequence of the war imposed upon them by the aggression of Germany and her allies.[21]

The Treaty of Versailles was not only devastating economically, it created tensions between different nationalities. Germany, for the most part, was disarmed; forbidden to have warplanes, tanks, or heavy artillery. The army was limited to 100,000 men. The treaty also required Germany to relinquish some territory. Part of Silesia was lost and East Prussia was cut off from the rest of Germany. West of the Rhine was to be a demilitarized zone and allied troops could occupy the west bank for fifteen years. The Central Powers' territory was divided up in a way that created social unrest. It was a socioeconomic disaster—new borders had separated raw material from manufacturers and producers from their markets, creating friction and hostility.[22] Many Germans found themselves in these new territories to be in the minority. With the mix of different nationalities, it became difficult to live together.[23]

Germany became a battleground for the war after the war—a civil war between nationalistic ex-soldiers and militant workers fighting over the future of Europe and its nation-states. The Weimar government became a model for postwar politics and social relations. However, it was severely lacking in genuine social

---

20. Keynes, *Economic Consequences of Peace*, ch. 5, sec. 2.
21. *Peace Treaty of Versailles*, clause 231.
22. Kagan et al., *Western Heritage*, 866.
23. Kagan et al., *Western Heritage*, 867.

The World Wars

change. This left a vacuum in Germany to be filled by antidemocratic political extremists. A combined philosophy of nationalist right and patriotic left resulted in National Socialism which contested Germany's future with democracy.[24] Germany's imperialist survivors patiently waited for their chance to implement a military philosophy and organize Germany's home front to do better in the next World War. The Treaty of Versailles created tensions between colonies and their ruling nations, resulting in serious instabilities. The Weimar government that ruled Germany until 1933, before Hitler assumed power, never overcame the stigma of accepting the Treaty of Versailles.[25] In the United States people became critical of the treaty because it seemed to contradict the idealistic and liberal philosophies the Western leaders had professed. It did not end imperialism. Some historians argued it overzealously promoted the national interests of the winning nations. It left groups of minorities outside the borders of their national homelands, violating the principles of national self-determination.[26]

The most outspoken delegate at the peace conference between the United States, France, and Britain was France's Georges Clemenceau. Clemenceau's main concern was the prevention of future German aggression against France; to ensure this he proposed measures that would weaken Germany's economy. Clemenceau expressed concern that Germany was never invaded or conquered, so its industrial capacity remained intact. He believed Germany's industrial base should be dismantled and the German economy should be restricted to a point where it could only focus on agriculture and small manufacturing. The German military should be reduced in size to provide defense only. Clemenceau also sought a military alliance between France, Britain, and the United States to protect against any possible German aggression. He was not a supporter of Wilson's Fourteen Points, which he saw as weak and lacking in chastizing measures against Germany. Initially, David Lloyd George of Britain adopted a more moderate position. He was

---

24. Kagan et al., *Western Heritage*, 869.
25. Philpott, *War of Attrition*, 350.
26. Kagan et al., *Western Heritage*, 868.

Philosophy of War

bothered by Wilson's Fourteen Points, because notions of self-determination were contradictory to Britain's control in the colonies and imperial assets. Lloyd George was in between Wilson's weaker approach and Clemenceau's harsh demands for retribution. In time his position hardened toward Germany, mainly because of the influence of Clemenceau and the anti-German press that swayed British public opinion demanding that Germany be punished.[27]

The peacemakers who met in Paris to decide Europe's fate still held imperialist views. The settlement was not without annexations or extreme indemnities. The League of Nations was formed. It was an international forum with the potential, but not the power, to keep the peace. The war had shattered societies but the worst was still to come. Disputed borders and social, economic, and political unrest created by the Treaty of Versailles resulted in a new ideological conflict which would threaten Europe until a second, more destructive, world war ensued in 1939.[28]

Comparing the Theories

There was not much discussion on strategy as it relates directly to conflict in this section. There is more to waging war than military engagements on the battlefield. The focus here was on monetary, foreign, and domestic policies. There are three primary existing factors relevant to the theorists' philosophies in this analysis. They are: Clausewitz's concept of total war through the mobilization of a nation's entire resources, specifically its citizens; Sun-tzu's monetary argument before committing to war; and Thomas Aquinas's warning against engaging in war for the purpose of gain. Clausewitz's vision of war was trinitarian. Clausewitz's trinity consisted of the following three elements: violence and passion, uncertainty and chance, and political purpose and effect. Violence and passion are the elements relevant to this section. According to Clausewitz, it is the task of political leaders to exploit the emotions of its citizens

27. Kagan et al., *Western Heritage*, 867.
28. Philpott, *War of Attrition*, 351.

during times of war.²⁹ Without the people's passion, war cannot be successfully waged. The Wilson administration understood this, hence their campaign of propaganda and rhetoric employed to persuade U.S. citizens into accepting the possibility of participating in the European war. After the Germans lost World War I, general Erich Ludendorff recognized German officials failed to mobilize the entire nation's resources, specifically the German people.³⁰

Sun-tzu warned against prolonged military campaigns. If the military is exposed to long conflicts, the state's resources will inevitably be depleted. Ultimately, this will have a negative impact on morale—thereby making success unachievable. "No country has ever profited from protracted warfare."³¹ The European Allies drove their countries deep into debt. When it became a possibility they may actually lose to Germany, the U.S. entered the war. However, it was not simply a call to war at the command of gold. If the U.S. financiers were unable to collect on the massive debt they had loaned to the European allies, it would have devastating consequences for the entire U.S. economy. It's likely the Wilson administration recognized this potential catastrophe looming and initiated a change in policy regarding neutrality. Perhaps one of the most significant lessons from this tragic war was Aquinas's philosophy on "just war," arguing that a nation must never wage war for gain. Further, war, according to Aquinas, does not belong to the private citizen. America's foreign policy seemed to distort this concept, considering the integrated role between private enterprise and government during the war.

The pretext for the First World War was the assassination of Austro-Hungarian heir Archduke Franz Ferdinand. This could have and should have remained a localized event.³² Two elements in Clausewitz's trinity provide insights for the true reasons for the Great War: the actions of the military (potential violence) and the passions of the people. First, the European powers were competing

29. Paret, "Clausewitz," 201.
30. Strachan, *Clausewitz's On War*, 19–20.
31. Sawyer, *Seven Military Classics of China*, 159.
32. Howard, *First World War*, 15.

over the modernization of their militaries; by some accounts, an arms race. Second, a Darwinian demeanor had infatuated the citizenry of the nations; many viewed warfare as a test of the nation's fitness for survival.[33] The assassination of Ferdinand, therefore, provided the European powers with a much-anticipated opportunity to unleash their passions and violence.

Origins of the Cold War

Before starting the next chapter, a review of the background on the Cold War may be prudent in order to provide a comprehensive understanding of the possessive clench communist ideology is capable of exerting on nations. There are many events that led to the Cold War. Some of the events that created tensions between the Soviets and the United States can be traced back before World War II officially ended. Eduard Mark has produced several publications on Soviet-American relations pertaining to the Cold War. He contends the United States was hoping to limit the control the Soviets had on their neighboring states. The U.S. policy was not to keep the Soviets from influencing their neighboring states but to keep them from dominating the region with the extension of the Soviet system through secret police.[34] However, the Soviets viewed this policy as a restriction on Soviet regime development in Eastern Europe. This led to further tensions as the U.S refused to recognize Bulgaria and Rumania. Stalin made it clear he did not care whether the U.S. recognized them and was not going to back away from exercising Soviet influence in the area.[35] The U.S. worried that a single power gaining dominance in Europe would threaten their national security, especially when considering the probability of Britain losing influence in the region. Still, the Soviets felt, as Secretary of State Byrnes put it, "ganged up on by the rest of the

---

33. Howard, *First World War*, 15, 27.
34. Mark Eduard, "American Policy Toward Eastern Europe," 327.
35. Mark Eduard, "American Policy Toward Eastern Europe," 328.

world."³⁶ The Soviets may have in fact been driven by these fears as the Americans did not object to the British imposing their chosen system of government in Greece.³⁷ However, British foreign policy resembled that of the Americans' when it came to promoting democracy and free societies, unlike the harsh draconian conditions communism inflicted upon its recipients.

The United States upheld their policy toward the Soviets. The goal was not to deny the Soviet Union authority as a great power in the region in relation to smaller countries but to limit internal influence on these smaller countries in the region. Mark argues there was cause for concern as Stalin intended to dominate the region, exercising control over all phases of the neighboring states. This debate bled over into the reconstructive process where the U.S. deliberated with the Soviets on a postwar loan. Thomas Paterson was president of The Society for Historians of American Foreign Relations and is affiliated with the University of Connecticut. According to Paterson, the Soviets were interested in American aid. However, the Americans attached stipulations and restrictions on the loan, making it a tool for diplomacy. In 1946, Paterson notes the United States gave aid to the British for reconstruction and argues that refusing to give similar aid to the Russians diminished the standard of living for the Russian people, created harsher Russian policies toward Eastern Europe, and damaged Soviet-American relations.³⁸ Both business and government leaders studied the possibilities of a loan to Russia and concluded the Russians would turn to America for materials needed to rebuild their war-torn economy and provide the Russian people with a higher standard of living. The treasury department officials also agreed the loan might benefit America's postwar economy, although not for the same reasons. Their key argument was the U.S. had suffered a depletion in raw material from the war that Russia could provide in exchange for credits. Still, Russia could only export these materials with the initial aid from the U.S. (developmental funds).³⁹

36. Mark Eduard, "American Policy Toward Eastern Europe," 328.
37. Mark Eduard, "American Policy Toward Eastern Europe," 324.
38. Paterson, "Abortive American Loan to Russia," 71.
39. Paterson, "Abortive American Loan to Russia," 74–75

Philosophy of War

Terms for the loan were never agreed upon. Washington's condition for loaning the funds was tied to Russia's behavior regarding international relations. Basically, Russia had to conduct their foreign policy according to American standards. Paterson's narrative seems to distort America's approach to diplomacy—using economics as a tool to enforce policy. Their decision not to loan money to Russia (without restrictions) did not expedite the Cold War. Paterson seems to place the blame solely on the Americans, citing Secretary of Commerce Henry Wallace, who believed the events set back the Soviets to their 1939 fears of capitalism and to the belief that the West, including the U.S., was invariably hostile.[40] However, these conclusions do not reflect the reality of Soviet ideology. It was the communist intent and part of their philosophy to spread communism around the globe to "rescue the proletariat." Considering this, it's doubtful an American loan without restrictions would have improved relations. Stalin would have completely dominated the region regardless. The upshot is Stalin was denied the funds the Americans could have provided him with to develop a stronger, possibly more aggressive Russia. Insights into the spread and aggressiveness of communist ideology are detected a few years prior in a different geographical area—Asia.

In the early twentieth century, when Japan occupied China, the Chinese's political leadership was struggling to unify China and rid themselves of their Japanese intruders. When Western powers turned them down, i.e., refused to provide them with assistance, they looked toward Eastern Europe. Russia's foreign minister, Leon Trotsky, was eager for the opportunity to spread the revolution abroad. In 1923, the Chinese Communist Party (CCP) was formed. Many communists joined the Nationalist Party, China's other political party, to form a united front against the intruders.[41] The two parties became suspicious of each other and after China's "War of Resistance against Japan" ended, their civil war began.[42] The Americans and Soviets were both reluctant to get involved;

---

40. Paterson, "Abortive American Loan to Russia," 87, 91.
41. Mitter, *Forgotten Ally*, 44.
42. Jian, *Mao's China & the Cold War*, 17.

both countries realized the situation in the region could escalate, resulting in war with each other. However, they also realized the strategic importance of the opposing country's influence on the region. The U.S. sent Marines to landing ports in the Northeast to support the Nationalist Party, and the Soviets promised the CCP aid and support for various other regions in China.[43] In 1945, the United States, the Soviet Union, Britain, France, and China met in London to discuss military control over Japan. When the Americans made it clear they alone would exercise authority in Japan, the Soviets responded by hardening their policy in China toward the United States.[44] As tensions intensified, Washington's only choice was to back the Nationalist Party in China. The conflict between two opposing political parties in China became an internal aspect of the emerging Cold War between the Soviets and the United States.[45] The Americans' decision to exercise sole authority in Japan was justified considering they were directly impacted by Japanese foreign policy (attack on Peral Harbor). Further, had the Americans been willing to share a role with the Soviets regarding Japan's future affairs, it would have materialized into a sharp divide, resulting in a much less democratic and free society. This statement is not hyperbole or conjecture; any doubt can be resolved by looking to Germany or Korea as evidence.

---

43. Jian, *Mao's China & the Cold War*, 31.
44. Jian, *Mao's China & the Cold War*, 31.
45. Jian, *Mao's China & the Cold War*, 36.

3

The Soviet-Afghan War

The Nuclear Age of Warfare

FOLLOWING WORLD WAR II, the new strategy the U.S. developed greatly diminished conventional warfare and became problematic. Nuclear weapons became the strategy rather than part of the strategic war plan. Years of relying on a strategy of mass nuclear retaliation first enacted by the Eisenhower administration weakened the conventional army. The fallacy of relying on the nuclear strategy became apparent to Harry G. Summers, an operations officer, during the Vietnam conflict. In 1975, before the fall of Saigon, Summers was in Hanoi negotiating the withdraw of U.S. personnel. A North Vietnamese official remarked how this war proved revolutionary ideals could not be stopped with force. Summers reminded his counterpart that nearly 800 years prior, Genghis Khan stopped a jihad against him in Central Asia by annihilating 10 million Muslims. Summers then reminded the North Vietnamese official the U.S. had more than enough nuclear weapons to completely destroy the country. The official replied, they were aware of this fact, but stated, "we also knew you would never use them."[1]

Industrialization led to advances in weapons—machine guns, longer-range artillery, etc.—resulting in a stalemate during WWI,

---

1. Summers, "Bankrupt Military Strategy," 34.

The Soviet-Afghan War

but only until they realized how to use the new weapons as a tool for advancement rather than as a strategy for war. The nuclear age seems to have made this mistake as well regarding new technology in the form of nuclear weapons.[2] These scenarios provided by history support Clausewitz's principles pertaining to war recorded in book eight of *On War* (i.e., holding strictly to the philosophical ideology of overthrowing the enemy brings war to its natural end, there is no other substitute or reality). Clausewitz's fundamental theory on war was it existed and served for the purpose of obtaining political goals—a means to an end. Absolute war was still a viable strategy developed in Clausewitz's trinity, exemplified in the conflicts of the nuclear age. Perhaps the Soviet-Afghan War best demonstrates the reality of Clausewitz's theories in the nuclear age. It also reveals the backlash governments face when unjustified wars are waged. The combined disregard for strategy and justification was catastrophic for the invaders.

In December 1979, the Soviet Union invaded Afghanistan.[3] One year prior, in April 1978, Afghanistan's government was overthrown by left-wing militants led by Nur Mohammad Taraki. After the successful coup, power was shared by two Marxist political groups—the People's Khalq Party and the Banner Parcham Party. The new government developed close relations with the Soviet Union and began a ruthless campaign against all domestic opposition, and at the same time they enacted new land and social reforms to support the new government's communist ideology.[4] The Soviets believed a military takeover would secure Afghanistan's place as a model for the Brezhnev Doctrine, proving that once a country became socialized Moscow would never permit it to return to capitalist standards.[5] This section covers the Soviet-Afghan War during the Cold War between the U.S and Russia. It discloses

2. Howard, *First World War*, 100.
3. Karp, "War in Afghanistan," 1026.
4. Editors of *Encyclopædia Britannica*, "Soviet Invasion of Afghanistan," para. 2.
5. United States Department of State, "Office of the Historian," preface, para. 6.

Philosophy of War

the danger of putting ideology before strategy, while demonstrating truths pertaining to the theories of absolute and limited war developed by Clausewitz.

The primary political groups in Afghanistan were Nationalist, Marxist, and Islamist until 1973, when Prime Minister Muhammad Daud overthrew his cousin King Zahir Shah in a coup and proclaimed himself president. According to Barnett Rubin—Professor of Political Science at Columbia University, rather than support a political faction, the United States and Soviet Union competed for influence over a regime they both supported. However, in April 1978, the People's Democratic Party of Afghanistan (PDPA), backed by the Soviet Union, seized power through a coup, killing the Prime Minister, and presented the Soviets with the opportunity to justify intervention.[6] Gregory Feifer is a former Moscow correspondent for National Public Radio. Feifer's interpretation of the Soviet-Afghan War supports Rubin's narrative regarding the Soviets' motivation for invading Afghanistan. He argues it was more than a simple act of aggression by a totalitarian state. The Cold War, Feifer contends, was the key factor in Moscow's decision to invade Afghanistan. They did not come to this decision hastily; according to Feifer, the Soviets had rejected pleas by Afghanistan's communist government for over a year to send troops to "help put down the rebellion," consisting of the rural population who were protesting the regime's modernization programs.[7] The Soviet leadership viewed Afghanistan's large Muslim population as a threat, fearing they would influence others to become anticommunist. The Soviets also claimed the Americans were planning an invasion, mostly to justify their own meddling in foreign affairs. Feifer argues the Soviets were oblivious to the political and cultural turmoil rampant in the country, and some of the Soviet officials were convinced by their own rhetoric of international duty to Afghanistan's proletariat. Soviet critics were astonished by the Kremlin's lack of foresight regarding similarities to Vietnam, and their inability to learn from America's failures in

---

6. Rubin, "Post-Cold War State Disintegration, 472–75.
7. Feifer, *Great Gamble*, 2.

The Soviet-Afghan War

the Vietnam War, which Moscow helped instigate.[8] Thus, blinded by ideology, the Soviets believed an invasion to prop up a proxy agent would increase their influence in the region, along with their status as a superpower in the world.[9]

In November 1979, the Soviet Interior Minister flew to Kabul to evaluate the Afghan Army. He prepared a report for Moscow, disclosing the dire conditions of the army—desertions and eroding discipline compelled him to request the Red Army be dispatched to the country immediately to stop the opposition from taking power.[10] After fierce debate the decision was made; Soviet troops began landing in Kabul airport in late December, followed by the 108th Motorized Rifle Division, invading from Termez with various other divisions and regiments in calculated locations throughout the country.[11]

Washington responded to the invasion in a less-than-desirable fashion. The Mujahideen was a sect of Islamic freedom fighters resisting the Soviets. The CIA funneled aid to this group through Pakistan's ISI. This was not ideal for the CIA, but it was easier than having to deal with several rebel groups and it helped camouflage Washington's role in the conflict.[12] In Congress, the primary supporter for jihad in Afghanistan was Texas Democratic Representative Charlie Wilson—an alcoholic playboy and former naval officer, according to Feifer. Wilson convinced Congress to increase spending to supply the Mujahideen. Soon, conservatives in Washington joined Wilson to support freedom fighters to battle what President Ronald Reagan called "the evil Empire." By 1985, spending for the Mujahideen, including funds diverted from the Pentagon to the CIA, reached $250 million. In April of that year, Reagan issued a directive requiring all available resources to go toward forcing the Soviets out of Afghanistan.[13]

8. Feifer, *Great Gamble*, 3.
9. Feifer, *Great Gamble*, 4.
10. Feifer, *Great Gamble*, 57.
11. Feifer, *Great Gamble*, 64.
12. Feifer, *Great Gamble*, 159.
13. Feifer, *Great Gamble*, 160.

Philosophy of War

The Russian General Staff examines, analyzes, and records lessons learned from conflicts. In 1995, the editors of this publication, Lester W. Grau and Michael A. Gress, learned the Soviet-Afghan War study had been conducted by the Russian General Staff but that it had not yet published it. The primary sources were extracted from the Archives of the Frunze Combined Arms Academy in Moscow, collected from officers who had served in Afghanistan. Grau is a retired Lieutenant Colonel in the U.S. Army, as well as a former Vietnam War veteran and military analyst. Gress is a former soldier in the motorized rifle forces of the Soviet Army. This analysis from the Russian General Staff provides insights into how the Soviets viewed their intervention in Afghanistan. They divide the Soviet-Afghan War into four phases, ranging from reason for intervention to the Soviets' departure. By not analyzing the conflict in the same manner as previous wars, they disclosed their bias regarding Marxist-Leninist ideology, which has some criteria for justifying war mostly dealing with revolutions against capitalism. Although the Russian General Staff is biased regarding justification, important intelligence records have been preserved from officers that served in the conflict. The Russian General Staff chooses to ignore some of the actions where no provisions exist within the Marxist-Leninist definition of just war. It shows the lack of defined political arrangements that determined the course of the conflict and the inabilities of the Soviet army to win decisively, affecting not only the Soviets' political structure but Russian society as well.[14]

The Soviets' obsession with spreading their ideology had a negative effect on their strategic operations from the beginning. For example, according to Feifer, there was confusion from the start; the Soviet leadership gave no clear orders to send troops into Afghanistan. Many Soviet officials were concerned only with the removal of Amin—a proxy agent for the Soviets who fell out of favor due to the suspicion he might decide to work with the Americans. When the KGB was finally successful in poisoning Amin, it was a Soviet doctor who revived him, revealing the lack

---

14. Russian General Staff, *Soviet Afghan War*, 12–14.

The Soviet-Afghan War

of coordination in operations. Essentially, Moscow was focused so intently on spreading communist ideology that they failed to construct a clear, laid-out objective that informed every critical branch of operating procedures related to combat objectives.[15]

The failure in strategic operations would eventually put stress on the Russian population as they continued to draft young men with no clear vision for ending the conflict. The stress manifested through the actions of draftees. For example, some young men were breaking their legs to avoid service or enrolling in school. However, the law changed, and college enrollment was no longer an acceptable pretext for evading service.[16] This is a revealing action of the unwillingness of Moscow to change direction when the war continued on the path of indefinite stagnation. Instead, Russian law was changed which allowed Moscow access to additional bodies so the communists could fulfill their international duty of, as Feifer stated, saving the proletariat in Afghanistan.[17]

In his publication, *Securing the Borders of Afghanistan During the Soviet-Afghan War*, Lester Grau disclosed why there were so many previous failed invasions of Afghanistan—because the country has limited access points due to natural barriers. This was counterintuitive for the Russians because they did attempt to control the borders by sealing them off. Still, small bands of fighters could avoid main points of entry. The terrain makes conditions ideal for the guerrilla warfare that the Mujahideen mastered. Grau points out the Soviets' initial mistake of preparing the Russian army for conventional warfare. Compared with the CIA's actions, supplying the Mujahideen with copies of the Qu'ran to give to the villagers near the Russian-Afghan border proved Washington had a clear, well-coordinated (although short-term) strategy for addressing the issues in Afghanistan. Most of the ethnic people in Afghanistan rejected modernization and communism; unlike the Soviets, who were using force to install their ideology, the CIA used Islamic culture to appeal to them not only through religion

---

15. Feifer, *Great Gamble*, 58–59, 70–71.
16. Tamarov, *Afghanistan*, 4, 11–16.
17. Feifer, *Great Gamble*, 3.

Philosophy of War

but by supplying them with arms as well.[18] In 1984, the CIA, in a joint operation with the Director General of Pakistani Inter-Services Intelligence (ISI) began a campaign of smuggling propaganda across the Amu Darya River to Soviet citizens. In 1985, the CIA discontinued the campaign, but ISI continued with the help of Mujahideen. The Mujahideen carried out attacks across the border in the Soviet Union, damaging an airfield and factory with rocket launchers. These actions resulted in Soviet officials paying a visit to Pakistan's Foreign Minister to make it clear any further attacks on Soviet soil would result in Pakistan being attacked by the Soviet Army.[19] By 1986, however, the Soviets were looking for an exit strategy in Afghanistan.[20] The lack of defined political arrangements that determined the course of the conflict and the inabilities of the Soviet army to win decisively affected not only the Soviets' political structure but Russian society as well, and losing the support of the Russian people helped motivate Moscow to look for a withdrawal.[21]

Azhar Javed Siddiqui and Khalid Manzoor Butts published an article in *A Research Journal of South Asians Studies*, arguing Afghan's ruling elite preferred a relationship with America over the Soviets. However, the U.S. preferred Pakistan over Afghanistan. The authors blame the U.S. for the war because of their reluctance to play a role. In 1946, Prime Minister of Afghanistan, Shah Mohammad Khan, "was convinced that the United States could guarantee his country's security," and he continued "not only to involve the United States in Afghanistan's economic development but also more importantly, to obtain U.S. support for the safeguarding of Afghanistan's political independence." Siddiqui and Butts criticized the United States foreign policy because the U.S. refused to act.[22] This is an unfair assessment because during this

---

18. Grau, "Securing the Borders of Afghanistan," 427.
19. Grau, "Securing the Borders of Afghanistan," 428.
20. Rubin, "Post-Cold War State Disintegration," 478.
21. Russian General Staff, *Soviet Afghan War*, xix.
22. Siddiqui and Butts, "Afghanistan-Soviet Relation During the Cold War," 619.

period the U.S. was under the Truman Doctrine and it was early in the Cold War. According to Michael Lind, author of *Vietnam: The Necessary War*, the Cold War emerged between two superpowers, the U.S. and Russia, following the end World War II. The threat of nuclear war prevented all-out war. War, therefore, was waged primarily through proxies in various parts of the world—Korea, Indochina, and Afghanistan. The Truman administration showed its resolve by going to war in Korea and extending military protection to Taiwan and French Indochina. The Truman Doctrine stated it was "the policy of the United States to support free people who are resisting attempted subjugation by armed minorities or by outside pressures."[23] Tensions were much higher in Korea during the time Siddiqui and Butts argued the U.S. should have done more to foster relations with Afghanistan. Following America's involvement in the Vietnam War, when the Cold War had moved to Afghanistan, the U.S. took the appropriate actions considering the lessons they learned from Vietnam and the reluctance of the American population to get involved in another foreign conflict. Even the Soviet critics point out the Kremlin's lack of foresight regarding Afghanistan because of America's failures in the Vietnam War that Moscow helped prolong.[24] In the Vietnam War, the initiative of global politics passed from the U.S. to the Soviets because Washington failed to establish a strategy for waging the Cold War in this location.[25] In Afghanistan, it seems the reversal was taking place between the two superpowers and the Soviets failed to recognize it because their ideology took preference to their military strategy.

Elisabeth Leake argues, in her article "The Great Game Anew: U.S. Cold-War Policy and Pakistan's North-West Frontier, 1947–65," Pakistan "become embroiled in the hegemonic struggle of the Cold War." The United States viewed Pakistan's North-West Frontier as strategically important and they became an ally. The United States's strategic vison regarding this frontier was threatened when Pakistan and Afghanistan began disputing over the area. Afghanistan

23. Lind, *Vietnam*, 5–6.
24. Feifer, *Great Gamble*, 3.
25. Lind, *Vietnam*,11.

Philosophy of War

continued to advocate for an autonomous zone comprised of the North-West Frontier that would share social, cultural, and political ties with Afghanistan known as Pakhtunistan. The Afghanis threatened to turn to the Soviets if they did not get their way, putting the United States in a precarious position between keeping their official alliance with Pakistan and preventing Afghanistan from aligning with the Soviets. The United States chose a neutral position that angered Pakistan and alienated Afghanistan.[26]

This weakens Siddiqui and Butts's claim that America's reluctance to play a role in Afghanistan resulted in turmoil in the region. The U.S. was clearly in a position where there was no good solution; unknowingly, and seeking a utilitarian position, they chose neutrality and antagonized both countries. It was the Soviets' actions that led to unrest in the region, further escalated by their misguided understanding of Afghanistan's national-historical factors. They considered any foreigner carrying weapons in their country as a threat that must be combated. By the time the Soviet High Command realized they would not be able to quickly suppress the Mujahideen because the primary issue was not military but political instability rooted in national-historical factors as described above, they had already been pulled deep into a civil war they did not comprehend. Moreover, the Afghan Army, supplied with Russian weapons, were mostly unreliable due to these historical and politically unstable conditions.[27]

In his publication, *Post-Cold War State Disintegration: The Failure of International Conflict Resolution in Afghanistan,* Rubin focuses on the failure of the U.N. to use its power of the Security Council to negotiate a solution regarding forming a State of Afghanistan. This was after the overthrow of the Soviet-backed government. Communism was declining in the country and democracy was being challenged by Islamic activists. However, there was disagreement among the activists over who was qualified to form and lead the government. Rubin argues the failure in conflict resolution resulted in chaotic skirmishes related to ethnic

---

26. Leake, "The Great Game Anew," 783–85.
27. Russian General Staff, *Soviet Afghan War,* 23.

The Soviet-Afghan War

divisions. More importantly, as communism diminished, and the Soviet-backed government was overthrown, democracy did not rise to become the primary principle in the politics of Afghanistan as the West had hoped. Islam become the social stratification the Afghans rallied to, making it nearly impossible for any form of representation to govern—democratic or otherwise.[28]

The invasion and overthrow of the Afghan government was the easy part. But soon the Soviet army was drawn into guerrilla warfare, fighting groups of insurgents throughout the country. The Soviets attempted to fight the way they had been trained—conventional warfare involving large-scale operations; they tried to adjust to the low-end tactical spectrum but the enemy would only fight when the terrain and odds were in their favor. According to the editors and translators of *The Russian General Staff*, Grau and Gress, the military leaders recommended a withdrawal but there was little help from the political masters. To further complicate the situation, General Secretary Leonid Brezhnev—leader of the Soviet Union, became incapacitated and took two years to die, leaving the Soviet Union without leadership from 1980–82. All decisions were made by a committee.[29] After Soviet leader Mikhail Gorbachev signed the Geneva Accords, to seek rapprochement with the United States, it allowed for the Soviet withdrawal of all troops from Afghanistan in February 1989.[30] The withdrawal of the Soviets created a vacuum Washington and its allies failed to properly address, leading to anti-American Islamic radicals.[31] Grau and Gress also argue the disillusionment in the communist system the Soviet soldiers brought home with them from the war spread to Soviet society, contributing to the Soviet Empire's collapse.[32]

28. Rubin, "Post-Cold War State Disintegration," 478.
29. Russian General Staff, *Soviet Afghan War*, xxiii.
30. Rubin, "Post-Cold War State Disintegration," 470–71.
31. Rubin, "Post-Cold War State Disintegration," 481.
32. Russian General Staff, *Soviet Afghan War*, xxv.

Philosophy of War

Comparing the Theories

The lack of defined political arrangements that determined the course of the conflict and the inabilities of the Soviet Army to win decisively affected not only the Soviets' political structure but Russian society as well, and losing the support of the Russian people pressured Moscow to look for an exit.[33] The actions by the Soviets in Afghanistan substantiates two of Clausewitz's theories on war: first, Clausewitz's fundamental theory on war was it existed for and served the purpose of obtaining political goals—a means to an end. The Russian General Staff point out in their analysis that a lack of defined political arrangements determined the course of the conflict and the inability of the Soviet Army to win decisively. Thus, the Soviets lacked a clearly defined political objective that was a fundamental aspect in Clausewitz's theories on war. Second was a recurring theme previously discussed in the World Wars section (Clausewitz's trinity "the people"). Russia's general population became disillusioned by the stagnating war and the demand for more of their young men each year. The growing dissatisfaction of the populists toward the Russian government for continuing the disastrous campaign in Afghanistan was precisely what Clausewitz warned against in the trinitarian element, "the people."

Finally, one of the major aspects that is sometimes controversial in Clausewitz's theory is clearly present in the Soviet-Afghan War—that is, limited war. There were so many previously failed invasions of Afghanistan because the country has limited access points due to natural barriers. The Russians attempted to control the borders by sealing them off. However, small bands of fighters could avoid main points of entry. The terrain makes conditions idea for the guerrilla warfare the Mujahideen mastered. The Soviets' initial mistake was attempting to fight the way they had been trained, i.e., conventional warfare involving large-scale operations. They tried to adjust to the low-end tactical spectrum, but the enemy would only fight when the terrain and odds were to their

---

33. Russian General Staff, *Soviet Afghan War*, xix.

advantage.[34] This was Clausewitz's meaning of limited war, not in the sense that it should be restricted by the command or political leaders, as was demonstrated in the Peloponnesian War by Athens, but that natural barriers can create conditions that restrict warfare, as was the case in the Soviet-Afghan War.[35]

This war was waged for ideological reasons. The Soviets were determined to extend their political views to other regions, and the U.S. was determined to contain or limit communist influence beyond a designated area (Eastern Europe). It was a proxy war during the Cold War between the United States and Russia. The U.S. managed to stay out of direct conflict. Instead, they managed to play a supportive role that was successful in limiting the spread of communist ideology. Further, the Americans were able to promote good and suppress evil, staying within the confines of Thomas Aquinas's theory on the justification to wage war. Of course, it's not surprising that neither the Russians nor the Afghans would consider Aquinas's theory on just war. Aquinas was a Westerner influenced by the Roman Catholic Church and Western philosophy. The Afghans were influenced by their Islamic religion and the Russians by communist ideology.

Conclusion

The reader can decide for themselves where to place limits on these theories. Thus, a formal conclusion will be withheld. Perhaps an argument can be made that financing a war is too near the equivalence of being directly involved. Providing loans for belligerent countries during the First World War led the U.S. to mobilization, but the financial entities were very different in the Soviet-Afghan War than they were for the Great War. Private enterprise provided financing for the Great War versus government financing for the Soviet-Afghan War. This can be tied to Aquinas's philosophy pertaining to war—that is, it does not belong to the private citizen,

---

34. Rubin, "Post-Cold War State Disintegration," 478.
35. Herberg-Rothe, "Primacy of 'Politics's or 'Culture,'" 178.

therefore only rulers charged with protecting the commonwealth have the moral authority to initiate war. Kagan's hypothesis regarding Athens' decision to take a limited stance is compatible with Clausewitz's theory in general on absolute war. The Soviets, however, were restricted to limited war in Afghanistan because of the terrain and the tactics their enemy chose to employ. A major blunder by the Soviets was the fact they had ignored the "people" element in Clausewitz's theory. Once the Soviet military lost the support of its citizens, it severely damaged communist ideology to the extent it never recovered in Russia. Nevertheless, it should be evident these theories are relevant for any duration of the past, present, or future. They function as a substrate on which complex social issues can be channeled; they are the anvil on which empires are forged. Perhaps for every empire war is inevitable, but when they disregard sound theories, as demonstrated in this analysis, they jeopardize their very existence.

Bibliography

Aquinas, Thomas. *Summa Theologica: On Law, Morality, and Politics*. Translated by Richard J. Regan. 2nd ed. Indianapolis, IN: Hackett, 2002.

Britannica Academic, s.v. "Carl von Clausewitz," https://academic-eb-com.ezproxy.liberty.edu/levels/collegiate/article/Carl-von-Clausewitz/24254.

Brown, John S. "Initially Reluctant, U.S." *Army Magazine* 67.4 (April 2017) 29.

Carey, Brian T. *Warfare in the Ancient World*. South Yorkshire, UK: Pen & Sword Military, 2013.

Clausewitz, Carl von. *On War*. Translated by J. J. Graham. New York: Barnes & Noble, 2004.

The Editors of *Encyclopædia Britannica*. "Soviet Invasion of Afghanistan." *Encyclopædia Britannica*. Last modified June 3, 2015. https://www.britannica.com/event/Soviet-invasion-of-Afghanistan.

Eduard, Mark. "American Policy Toward Eastern Europe and the Origins of the Cold War, 1941–1946." *The Journal of American History* 68.2 (September 1981) 313–36. http://www.jstor.org/stable/1889975.

Erickson, Millard J. *Christian Theology*. 3rd ed. Grand Rapids: Baker Academic, 2013.

Evans, Stephen C., and R. Zachary Manis. *Philosophy of Religion: Thinking about Faith*. 2nd ed. Downers Grove, IL: InterVarsity, 2009.

Feifer, Gregory. *The Great Gamble: The Soviet War in Afghanistan*. New York: Harper Perennial, 2010.

Grau, Lester W. "Securing the Borders of Afghanistan During the Soviet-Afghan War." *Journal of Slavic Military Studies* 28.2 (January 2015) 414–19, 427.

Handel, Michael I. "Corbett, Clausewitz, and Sun Tzu" *Naval War College Review* 53.4 (Fall 2000) 106–24.

Hanlon, Michael E. "America's Turn from Neutrality to Intervention, 1914–1917." *Relevance* 1.2 (Spring 1992) 178–79.

Herberg-Rothe, Andreas. "Primacy of 'Politics' or 'Culture' Over War in a Modern World: Clausewitz Needs a Sophisticated Interpretation." *Defense Analysis* 17.2 (2001) 175–86. http://www.dtic.mil/dtic/aulimp/citations/gsa/2001_112382/1925.html.

Horn, Martin. "A Private Bank at War: J.P. Morgan & Co. and France, 1914–1918." *The Business History Review* 74.1 (Spring 2000) 85–112.

Bibliography

Howard, Michael. *The First World War: A Very Short Story.* New York: Oxford University Press, 2007.

Jian, Chen. *Mao's China & the Cold War.* Chapel Hill, NC: University of North Carolina Press, 2001.

Kagan, Donald. *On the Origins of War: And the Preservation of Peace.* New York: Anchor, 1995.

Kagan, Donald, et al. *The Western Heritage.* Upper Saddle River, NJ: Pearson Prentice Hall, 2007.

Karp, Craig M. "The War in Afghanistan." *Foreign Affairs* 64.5 (Summer 1986) 1026–47.

Keynes, John. *The Economic Consequences of Peace.* The Project Gutenberg eBook on the Web, May 1920. https://www.gutenberg.org/files/15776/15776-h/15776-h.htm.

Leake, Elishabeth. "The Great Game Anew: U.S. Cold-War Policy and Pakistan's North-West Frontier, 1947–65." *The International History Review* 35.4 (2013) 783–806.

Lind, Michael. *Vietnam: The Necessary War.* New York: Touchstone, 2002.

Lonsdale, David J. "Ordering and Controlling the Dimensions of Strategy," *Defense Studies* 16.4 (2016) 399–400. https://doi.org/10.1080/14702436.2016.1228430.

McGrath, Alister E. *Historical Theology: An Introduction to the History of Christian Thought.* 2nd ed. Oxford: Wiley & Sons, 2013.

Mitter, Rana. *Forgotten Ally: China's World War II, 1937–1945.* New York: Houghton Mifflin Harcourt, 2014.

Paret, Peter. "Clausewitz." In *Makers of Modern Strategy: From Machiavelli to the Nuclear Age,* edited by Peter Paret, 186–213. Princeton: Princeton University Press, 1986.

Paterson, Thomas G. "The Abortive American Loan to Russia and the Origins of the Cold War, 1943–1946." *The Journal of American History* 56.1 (January 1969) 70–92.

Peace Treaty of Versailles. http://net.lib.byu.edu/~rdh7/wwi/versa/versa7.html.

Philpott, William. *War of Attrition: Fighting the First World War.* New York: Overlook, 2015.

Pinckaers, Servais, et al. "Ethics and the Image of God." In *The Pinckaers Reader: Renewing Thomistic Moral Theology,* edited by Berkman John and Titus Craig Steven, 130–43. Washington, DC: Catholic University of America Press, 2005.

Rubin, Barnet R. "Post-Cold War State Disintegration: The Failure of International Conflict Resolution in Afghanistan." *Journal of International Affairs* 46.2 (Winter 1993) 472–75.

The Russian General Staff. *The Soviet Afghan War: How a Superpower Fought and Lost.* Edited and Translated by Lester W. Grau and Michael A. Gress. Lawrence: University Press of Kansas, 2002.

Sawyer, Ralph T. *The Seven Military Classics of China.* New York: Basic, 2007.

Bibliography

Siddiqui, Azhar J., and Khalid Manzoor Butts. "Afghanistan-Soviet Relation During the Cold War: A Threat for South Asian Peace." *A Research Journal of South Asian Studies* 29.2 (December 2014) 619.

Special to *The New York Times*. (1936, Jan 11). "J. P. Morgan Denies Letting the Pound Slip to Force 1915 Loan." *New York Times (1923-Current File)*. ProQuest. http://ezproxy.liberty.edu/login?qurl=https%3A%2F%2Fwww.proquest.com%2Fdocview%2F101961739%3Faccountid%3D12085.

Strachan, Hew. *Clausewitz's On War: A Biography*. New York: Grove, 2007.

Summers, Harry G. "A Bankrupt Military Strategy: Our Military Assets Can No Longer Cover Our Foreign-Policy Liabilities." *Atlantic* 263.6 (June 1989) 33–37, 40.

Tamarov, Vladislav. *Afghanistan: A Russian Soldier's Story*. Translated by Naomi Marcus, et al. Berkeley, CA: Ten Speed, 2001.

"The Image of God." *Life of the Spirit* 6.61 (1951) 27–29.

Thucydides. *The Peloponnesian War*. Translated by Martin Hammond. New York: Oxford University Press, 2009.

United States Department of State. "Office of the Historian, Bureau of Public Affairs." Last modified May 4, 2017. https://history.state.gov/historicaldocuments/frus1977-80v12/preface.

Widen, J. J. "Sir Julian Corbett and the Theoretical Study of War," *Journal of Strategic Studies* 30.1 (Winter 2007) 109–27. https://doi.org/10.1080/01402390701272533.

Zieger, Robert H. *America's Great War: World War I and the American Experience*. New York: Rowan & Littlefield, 2001.

www.ingramcontent.com/pod-product-compliance
Lightning Source LLC
Chambersburg PA
CBHW061515040426
42450CB00008B/1636